# Words that Name Things

girl

THE DANBURY PRESS
a division of Grolier Enterprises Inc.
Publisher: Robert B. Clarke

Copyright © 1976 The Walt Disney Company
Original 4 volume concept by Vincent H. Jefferds.
Made and printed by Purnell and Sons Limited
Paulton (Avon) and London

Second U.S. Edition 1978
Library of Congress Catalog Card Number: 76-19204

ISBN: 7172-8114-0

Printed in 1990

shirt

dwarf

# Walt Disney's
# Words that Name Things

**THE DANBURY PRESS**

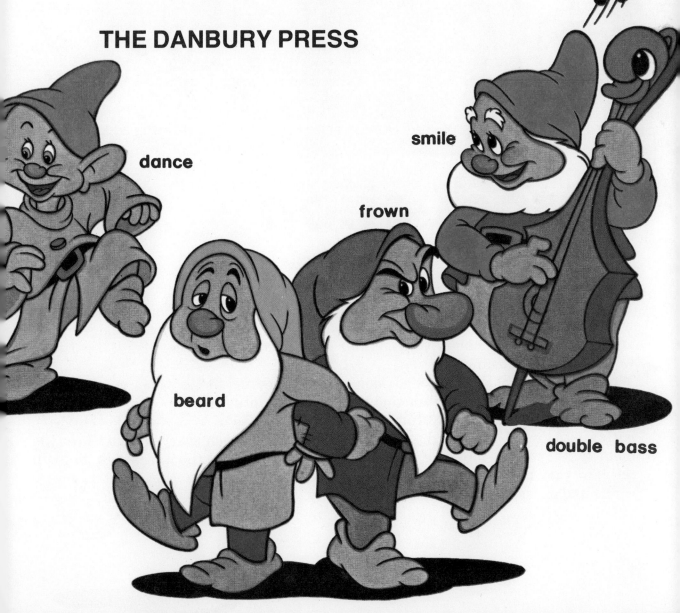

dance

smile

frown

beard

double bass

pretty paintings

guns

rocking-horse

hobby-horse

two curious children

very old sea-chest

valuable chair

real oak table

# Introduction

## A Note to Parents

Why do your children need books about words? Perhaps they are already at school, learning new words every day. The answer is that while they may not be ready for any more books just about words, children do need help in recognizing the uses of words they are learning.

WORDS! WORDS! WORDS! has been specially created to increase the vocabulary of the young child in an original and highly entertaining way.

We have produced a four-volume picture book series of first words for children, with a picture for *every* word, and a pictorial setting which every child will readily identify. When they look at a page they will not only learn the words on it, but will see how they are used, what they describe or name, and how they relate to other words and phrases which they hear every day.

priceless
painting

bookcase

store clerk

old
storekeeper

parcel

stool

oks

baby's cradle

customer

excitable dog

Each volume is about a different word classification — nouns, verbs, adjectives and adverbs, opposites — and every page contains a key word around which the visual theme revolves. The key words have been carefully selected by educational experts from vocabulary lists of the word range for young children. New, related words are then introduced on the page, so that children soon find that they have at their command a whole range of words, together with a visual understanding of their meanings and use, which they can relate to their own experience.

With the help of these delightful books your children will absorb information in an effortless and pleasurable way, with all the best-loved Disney characters as their companions.

This book is about the names of things and teaches children to identify the things they see around them.

To add to the fun of learning, there are also a number of amusing games and puzzle pages.

flipper

goggles

snorkel

plum pudding

holly

diver

chef

painter

# Contents

nurse

ladder

day tripper

sailor

telescope

cowboy

astronaut

rocket

lasso

policeman

fireman
and hose

teacher

# Party

balloon

Captain Owl

great-great-great-great
Grandpa Pooh

Christopher Robin
dressed up
as Peter Pan

mandolin

vegetar
gu

piano

accordion

Pirate Pooh

wooden
sword

cracker

whistle

swe

piano stool

8

big balloon

paper decorations

balloonist pirate
(hold on tight!)

great-great-great-great
Grandma Pooh

Lady Pirate

Pirate Eyore
getting scared

paper hat

cake and candles

paper hat

jelly

Tiggers like cake best

9

# Family

great-great-uncle

grandad

grandma

uncle

aunt

cousin

sister

Donald

10

Donald's family tree

# Television

pictures of television stars

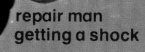

repair man getting a shock

television giving trouble

plug

antenna socket

tools

television schedule

small viewers

antenna

ladder for fixing antenna on roof

TV

repair man's truck

ack

television program

tv tray

cabinet

controls

screen

a happy viewer

portable television

13

# Wedding

church

relations

confetti

groom's father

veil

bride's mother

bouquet

bridegroom

ring

ribbons

bride

page boy

friends of bride

14

best man

bride's father

preacher

idesmaid

camera

photographer

usher

15

# Birthday

birthday boy

music makers

BALOO

drum

guitar

straw

lemon

giving a
present

birthday food

fruit

chocolate cookies

candy

a hungry
guest

singers

dancers

candle

birthday cake

-cream

jelly

birthday cards

ckers

n pastry

17

# Dodging

Help the three little pigs get to the brick house and es[cape]
the tricks of the Big Bad Wolf. You need three cou[nters]
and a dice. Choose which character you would like t[o be]
and throw a six to start and the exact number to finish.

**Start**

1  2  3  4  5  6  7  8  9

Big Bad Wolf has put some
boulders on the path and blocked
it. Miss three goes moving them

10  11  12  13  14  15  16  17  18  19

Take a short cut
from 11 to 17

18

the Baddie

Attacked by Big Bad Wolf. Go back to 28

32
33
34

31
30
29
28
35

36

27
37

39
38

26

40

41

25
42

Big Bad Wolf uses a trip rope. Go back to 35

43

24

23

44

22

21
45

Finish

ake a short
ut to 39

mbushed by
ig Bad Wolf.
o back to 14

19

# Circus

trapeze artist

bareback
rider

whoops!

parasol

plumes

horse

performing elephant

circus ring

sawdust

20

trapeze

tightrope walker

beautiful costume

audience

top hat

whip

clown

box

Ringmaster

red nose

he won't be laughing much longer

21

# Carnival

ferris wheel

caravans

side shows

ring-toss stall

fortune
teller

crystal
ball

candy
apple
seller

hot dogs

cotton
candy

merry-go-round

CAN

COTT

24

vulture

monkey

**Zoo**

TIGER

snake

man cub

Please do not
feed the animals

wolf cubs

elephant

ap

26

baby elephant

woodpecker

crocodile

chipmunk

bear

LION

SNAIL

Danger — man-eater!

monkeys

27

# Theater

spotlight

curtains

sand b[ox]

audience

produc[er]

box

Cinderella
Act 4

sh[ow]
ca[rd]

front
row

balcony

28

flies

backdrop

props

actresses

stage hand

footlights

critic

stage

box

29

# Beach

seagull

pier

sea

sand dunes

rocks

boat

beach ball

surfboard

wave

ice-cream

cone

windbreak

car inner tube

spade

bucket

sandcastle

starfish

lobster

shrimp

ky

ICES

cliffs

steps

beach boy

umbrella

wet bathing trunks

and

shadow

wel

beach house

ing net

sunglasses

popsicle

shells

deckchair (collapsing)

31

# Barbecue

smoke

burnt
hot dog

fork

grill

charcoal

brick barbecue

plate

pepper

plate

bread

rude bird

baked potatoes

soup

king-size
sandwich

barbecued
carrot

33

# Camp

farmhouse

barn

clothes line

washing

water carrier

ridge tent

tent pole

guy rope

frying pan

troop leader

stove

tent peg

BEANS

34

apple picking

frame tent

field

ladder

sleeping bag

groundsheet, being folded

old boot

cooking pot

fishing for supper

camp fire

camp stool

happy camper

stream

35

# River

meadow

onlooker

footbridge

fishing net

water

reflection

dragonfly

jar for minnows

buttercup

two fish

grass

36

# Day

Sunday

minister

bible

pulpit

Christmas Day

Santa Claus

chimney

Easter Day

broken egg

bucket and spade

luggage

holiday

600117

38

**weekday**

ff to school

satchel

sack full of
nice presents

**birthday**

birthday
boy

HAPPY
BIRTHDAY

presents

clothes
pins

clothes
line

**washday**

line prop

washing

ost

apron

clothes basket

39

# Christmas

teddy bear

little boys who
should be asleep

trumpet

toy
soldier

stocking

guitar

train engine

book

pillowcase

40

chimney

sleigh

a tired reindeer

candle

ball

Santa Claus

sack full of presents

drumsticks

drum

more presents

boots to keep
Santa's feet warm

lasso to trap Santa Claus

41

**eauty**

**19** Pass by Maleficent Go to 22

**20**

**21**

**18**

**22**

**17**

**23** Good Fairy Go forward 10 places

**16**

**24**

## Rules

A game for any number of players
Throw a 6 to start
Throw an exact number to finish

**15**

**25**

**14**

**26**

**13**

**27**

**10** Secret stairway Go to 33

**9**

**11**

**12** Lost sword Go back to Start

**34** Go up the steps to 9

**33**

**32**

**31** Lost in magic cave Miss a turn

**30**

**29**

**28**

**Finish**

**68**

**67** Raven on guard Go back to Forest of Thorns

**66**

**43**

# Playground

slide

wheeeeeeee!

sand bo[x]

pogo stick

ball

pond

toy boat

44

kite

lovely fun

swing

hula hoop

see-saw

No Ball Games

soccer ball

jump rope (not being used for jumping)

45

# Soccer

stand

ticket
collector

injured player

rattle

supporters

club manager

successful
kick

home team

team uniform

46

# Game

jumping

Jump rope

snakes and ladders

cap

swag bag

mask

dice

counter

feather

headband

cowboys and Indians

stetson

bow

necktie

arrow

gun and holster

48

blind man's buff

blindfold

police cap

policeman's club

roller skate

histle

ps and robbers

leap frog

tree stump – a good place
to hide behind!

hide and seek

49

# Fun

cone

ice-cream

Indian

feathered
head-dress

rein

paint

arrows

bow

rocking-horse

road

ball

cloud

balloon

hat

butterfly net

piggy-back ride

scarf

butterfly

fence

driver

hungry passenger

mane

snack

cart

ribbon

wheel

toadstools

51

# Sports Day

three legged race

sack race

losers falling over

sack

obstacle race

tire

referee

3

4

cheat! — you should
go over the fence

52

stop watch

Mr. Timekeeper

finishing tape

tied legs

competitor's number

spoon

broken egg

egg and spoon race

groundsheet

# Snowman

pile of snowballs

old top hat

stones for eyes and mouth

carrot for nose

slide

pipe

snowman

never turn your back when playing snowballs!!

playing hide and seek

54

snowflakes

fir trees

snowplough

woolly pom-pom hat

making
a snowball

woolly
scarf

snowdrift

# Mountain

heaven

avalanche

ski jumper

gogg[les]

ski pole

parka

Saint Bernard dog

tea →

sk[i]

ice axe

WATCH YOUR STEP

river b[ed]

tent

rope

rescue helico[pter]

icicles

Swiss cheese

climbing boots

snow

base c[amp]

56

peak

mountain range

roping down

rucksack

cloud

itt

rock climbers

100% wool

mountain goat

ledge

lacier

atermelon

eyrie

steps cut into the ice

57

# Parachute

sky divers with colored smoke

parachute canopy

pilot chute

pilot ejecting from diving airplane

airfield

shrouds

basket

jumpsuit

goggles

rip cord

parachute harness

landing target

jumpers

airplane

cloud

parachute
pack

lots of
parachutes

helmet

landing!

duck pond

take-off

# Picture

By copying the illustrations of the characters on this page, you can fill in the blanks on the opposite page, to complete the picture

**Piglet**

**Rabbit**

**Eyore**

**Christopher Robin**

**Winnie the Pooh**

**Tigger**

**Owl**

**Roo**

**Kanga**

# Home

wigwam

fierce bear

whoops!

Indian

igloo

gipsy caravan

lovely smell

gipsies

earri

camp fire

62

club

caveman

cave

yesterday's dinner!

bricks of ice

palm leaf roof

Eskimo

mud hut

bricks of mud

tribesman

hole in the ice
to fish through

friend

63

# School

blackboard with lesson on it

globe

chair

pegs

easel

note p[ad]

naughty
pupil
standing
on stool

pencil sharpener

pencils

eraser

pen and ink

decorated jar

storybook

waste basket

desk

very
young
pupil

pieces
waste pap[er]

stool

text book

blot of ink

wall clock

window

mortar board

picture painted by artistic pupil

Principal

paint palette

hand bell

paint brushes

box of rubber bands

pupil giving an excuse

sheets of paper

cane

scissors

spilt paint

ruler

exercise book

bookcase

paste

thumb tacks

microscope

eager pupil choosing book

65

# Factory

hoist

stores

workshop

goggles

pow
dri

steel

welder

loading bay

storeman

timber

acetylene cylinder

tool box

fi

cans of paint

paint sprayer

spray gun

wheelbarrow

overalls

spray booth

conveyor belt

leve

paint drying machine

# Building

Romeo

chimneys

roof

pennants

turret

Juliet

look-out

inn sign

inn

stone seat

castle

moat

thatched roof

drawbridge

garden

cottage

gate

68

cooling towers

smoke stack

weather cock

tower blocks

factory

warehouse

steeple

gable

HOTEL

window panes

canopy

tower

pavement

stone wall

church

churchyard

69

Street

lights

meat market

stores

truck

store window

angry driver

sports car

shopper

fire hydrant

baby carriag

pedestrian crossing

corner

road surface

manhole

lane markings

70

road signs

stop

traffic lights

bookstore

taxi

double
yellow lines

policeman

pedestrian

traffic
control
button

pavement

curb

drain

71

# Garage

sign

gasoline tanker

highway

car wash

headlight

foam

radio

tow truck

gas pump

hook

water

jack

apprentice mechanic

air hose

engi

grease

cans of oil

grease gun

chief mechanic

lugwrenc

rear window

handle

extra passenger

oor

tch

wheel

fender

trunk

rear light

hub

axle

ramp

puncture

wrench

mechanic

new exhaust

nuts

new tires

73

# Station

train leaving
station

signal

lamp

newsstand

green flag

whistle

guard

passenger
going on
vacation

suitcase

train

crate

LIVE
STOCK

THIS WAY UP

parc

WAY OUT

station clock

bulletin board

TRAVEL BY RAIL TO_

TRAIN PARTURES

timetable

TICKETS

ticket office

HOT DRINKS

COFFEE
TEA
SOUP

station seat

station master

ket and spade

ticket

ticket collector

trunk

porter

hot drinks machine

luggage cart

75

# Train

signals

early American locomotive

Stephenson's Rocket

fireman

driver

foreman

coffee

maintenance man

rail

brazier

book of tickets

ticket clerk

wicked villain

norail train

diesel locomotive

electric train

changing the points

shunter

buffers

EXIT

subway train

watch
the doors

:ket or your life . . .'

platform

77

# Seaport

lighthouse

lifeboats

portholes

anchor

oil tanker

sails

harbor

fishing boat

buoy

ocean liner

wooden crates

mast

funnel

HANDLE WITH CARE

sailor

wheel

life belt

fender

tug boat

sea

# Airport

helicopter

hangar

anothe
mechan

smuggler

light aircraft

CUSTOMS

prope

fuel tanker

AVGAS

jet plane being refuelled

fuselage

tail

win

steps

passengers

stewardess

80

runway

jet plane taking off

radar dish

wind indicators

baggage cart

air traffic controller — a very important person

control tower

airport manager

pilot

mechanic

jet engine

sightseers

# Boat

ocean liner

cabin cruiser

cockpit

stern

amidships

hull

inflatable dinghy

home made boat

scull

paddle

flying boat

handrails

mast

deck

bow

sail

Daisy Belle

WAYFARER

sailing dinghy

ARROWHEAD

49

outboard motor

speedboat

83

# Mill

slates

spur wheel

windmill

trough

mousetr

water wheel

wooden crown wheels

chu

flou

stuck duck

flour sacks

84

stream

ear wheel

clutch

shaft

sack
hoist

hook

rope

grain

hopper

millstone

mill hands

miller

wooden
steps

watermill

grain sacks

thieves

85

# Palace

grand duke

crown

royal treasury

throne

king

stairway to treasury

royal cook making cakes for king's tea

palace kitchen

secret hoard

fresh fruit

...ting of part of royal kingdom
...nknown artist  working in stables)

eautiful
rincess

handsome
prince

footman
(bored to tears)

turret

royal wine cellar

main staircase

...l, taking
...ing's
...shments

# Maze

Can you help Alice
find the right path
through the maze?
She wants to reach
her sister on the
river bank

89

# Supermarket

cashier

store manager

beans

peas

cash register

detergent

conveyor belt

mustard

checkout counter

bread

shopping basket

WASHING POWDER

Mustard

cocoa

honey

peaches

FRUITS & VEGETABLES

salt

cheese

jam

coffee

peanut butter

EN FO

mburgers

sausages

cken

tea

SUGAR

freezer

TEA

FLOUR

BUTTE

cereal

CORN FLAKES

shopper

cart

rail

91

# Fruit

grapes

fruit sta[tion]

scales

bags

pencil
behind ear

fruit boxes

pears

plums

salesman

pineapples

raspberries

92

bananas

apples

peaches

oranges

coin

customer

strawberries

hand cart

93

# Vegetables

green beans

asparagus

cucumbers

price tag

brussels spro

shelf

grocer

weig

scales

eggplants

counter

customer

squash

shopping basket

articho

onions

pers

tomatoes

carrots

OPEN

potatoes

cauliflowers

greedy customers

lettuces

95

# Kitchen

containers

Tea Coffee Sugar

shelf

kitchen utensils

scales

dirty dishes

faucets

sink

washing machine

wooden spoon

mixing bowl

cupboar

apron

fo

k

bag of flour

spoon

can opener

butter

tablecloth

stool

96

plates

cups and saucers

dish

milk

freezer

warming rack

frozen foods

dishwashing liquid

saucepan
boiling

refrigerator

frying
pan

pepper mill

casserole

hotplate

salt shaker

oven
gloves

stove

pepper shaker

oven
door

dish towel

SALT

JSA D

99

# Garden

apple trees

greenhouse

hedge

garde

seedlings

watering can

wheelbarrow

flowers

rose

bee

butterfl

98

smoke

fence

vegetable patch

onfire

blackbird

bird feeder

spider

goldfish
pond

statue
with fountain

garden path

lawn

rock garden

sleeper
(gardener's assistant)

trowel

rug

99

# Boxes

work box

treasure chest

paint box

tool bo

crayon box

surprise box

egg box (falling)

cookie box

cereal box

money box

chocolate box

shoe box

hat box

musical box

toy box

jack-in-the-box

# Clothes

**Summer Clothes**

blouse

pleated skirt

sandals

hat

boots

coat

mittens

bow

dress

shoes

**Undercloth**

petticoat

panties

tights

bathrobe

pretty nightgown

mule slippers

Night Cloth

Winter Clothes

Summer clothes (again)

blazer

scarf

storm coat

pom-pom hat

tee-shirt

shorts

woolly jumper

undershirt

underpants

socks

shirt

pyjamas

trousers

dressing gown

shoes

slippers

103

# Bathtime

shaving mirror

toothbrushes

mug

soap

toothpaste

face cloth

wash basin

bathroom stool

nailbrush

tiles

bathbrush

bathrobe

towel bar

towels

snorkel

face mask

faucets

nice hot water

bath

bubbles

toy boat

soggy, wet sponge

slippers

bathmat

# Bedtime

window

picture

moo[...]

night-light

tablecloth

rug

favorite toy train

floorboards

curtains

Mummy

storybook

bed

pillow

sheets

pajamas

slippers

patchwork
quilt

# Haunted House

Can you help Robin Hood to find his way out of the haunted house? The only rule is that you can't walk through walls

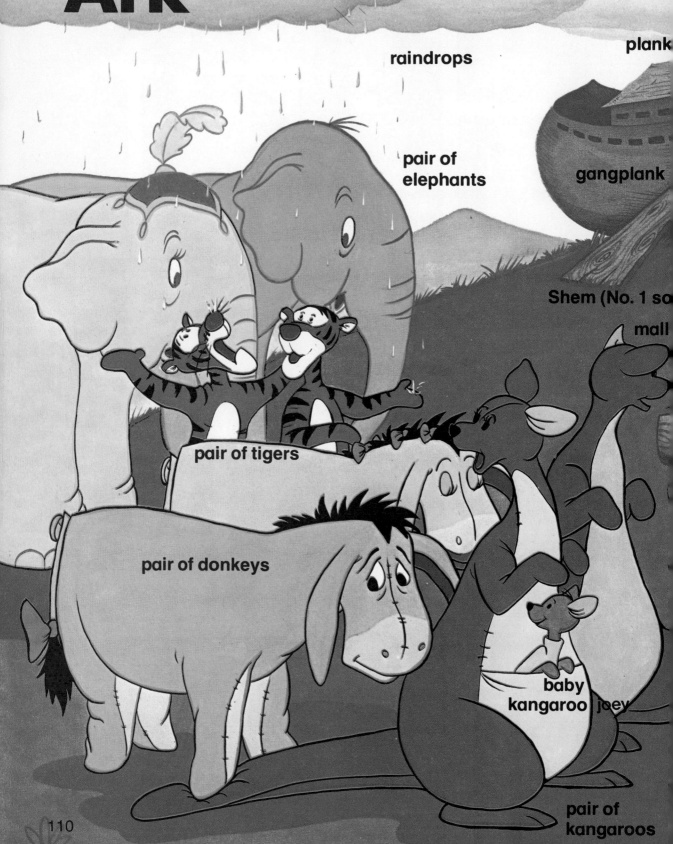

# Ark

rain clouds

plank

raindrops

pair of
elephants

gangplank

Shem (No. 1 so

mall

pair of tigers

pair of donkeys

baby
kangaroo joey

pair of
kangaroos

110

olive branches

Mount Ararat

adder

pair of doves

ewdriver

logs

40 DAY
PACKAGE
HOLIDAY
Wait here

Ham
(No. 2 son)

ark plans

thumb tacks

pencil

s

king planks

table

Japheth
(No. 3 son)

check
list

money bag

Mr Noah

Mrs Noah

money

111

# Rain

drainpipe

drip

gutter

lady's umbre

very deep puddle — nice and splashy

small shelter

dog shaking off water

drain

112

storm clouds

downpour

lightning

raindrops

toy boat

see-through umbrella

souwester

raincoat

rubber boots

a naughty splash

113

# Wind and Sun

very strong wind

old hat swept away i
gust of wind

windblown hiker

swirling leaves

trees bending
in the wind

tunic

little friend of hiker

114

happy, smiling sun

mother bird and babies

nest

singing bird

beads of sweat

butterfly

stone wall

knapsack

staff

toadstools

very warm peasant under shady tree

# Stars

inside the observatory

planetary observation chart

giant telescope

globe

alien

astronomer

observation platform

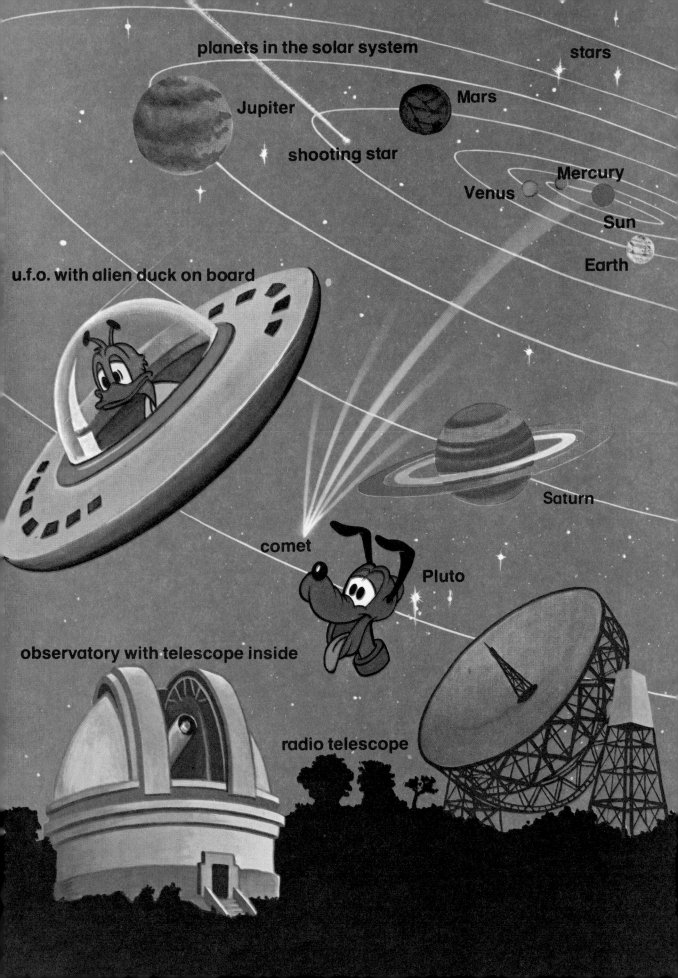

# Mix up

All these characters have got the wrong bodies, and some have even got the wrong feet. Can you sort them out?

Bambi O–U; Dopey Q–B; Pluto T–P; Mickey V–D

fisherman's boat

splash!

sky

waves

message in a bottle

Sea

young fishes

bad tempered crab

air bubbles

rigging

face mask

excited sand fisherman

makeshift fishing rod

glug!

shipwreck

flippers

starfish

baby turtle

hermit crab

old tin can

120

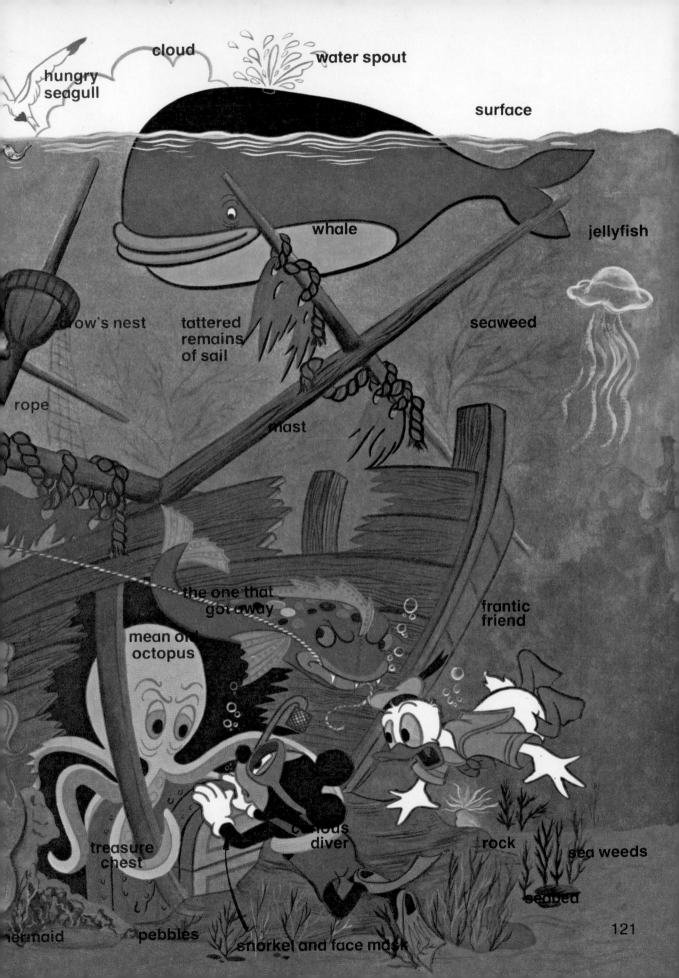

hungry
seagull

cloud

water spout

surface

whale

jellyfish

crow's nest

tattered
remains
of sail

seaweed

rope

mast

the one that
got away

frantic
friend

mean old
octopus

treasure
chest

curious
diver

rock

sea weeds

seabed

mermaid

pebbles

snorkel and face mask

121

# Bird

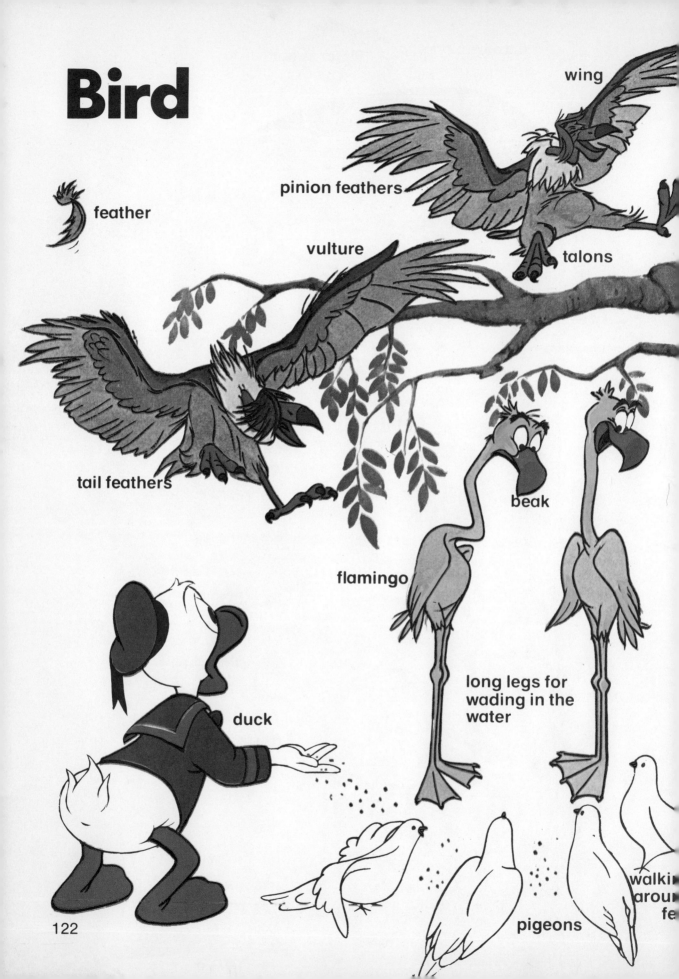

feather

wing

pinion feathers

talons

vulture

tail feathers

beak

flamingo

long legs for wading in the water

duck

pigeons

walki
arou
fe

bright eyes for
seeing at night

raven

ostrich

owl

perching
feet

silly little wings!
no good
for flying

parrot

long legs
for running

goose (very silly)

crow

123

webbed feet for swimming

# Mothers and Babies

puppy

ostrich
egg

gos...

sheep (ewe)

lamb

rabbit (doe)

kangaroo

baby rabbit

joey

# Monster

horns

helmet

brave knight

sharp teeth

webbed wings

armor

hot breath

Prince Charming

sword

shield

lance

trusty steed

frightened horse

EXCITING ISN'T IT?

sign

turret

princess in distress

dragon

claws

hero

arrows

arless
uck

baddies

seeing
stars

# Tree

chestnut tree

wasps' nest

owl

wasps

owlet

woodpecker

bark

grub

trunk

hollow

hibernating hedgehog

rabbit

eart

worm

roots

worm holes

horse chestnut in prickly case

autumn leaves

crow

squirrel

nut

bird's nest

nch

twig

Davy Crockett hat

falling leaves

lumberjack

lumberjack's jacket

trees

field

denim jeans

sapling (baby tree)

axe

oots

bit warren

sleeping rabbit

129

# Light

moonlight

sodium lamp

POLICE   PD

traffic lights

street
light

warning beacon

bicycle light

road
lamp

headlight

turn indicator

130

COP 1

ceiling light

nightlight

candle

standing lamp

flashlight

porchlight

table lamp

firelight

CAFÉ

131

# Mine

prop

miner's
helmet

gallery

spoil

tub

diamonds

pail

foreman

manager

133

# Rescue

**A dice and counter game for up to eight players**

The Prince and the Seven Dwarfs are trying to rescue poor Snow White, but her wicked stepmother is trying to stop them. Pretend to be one of the rescuers and see if you can win by rescuing her. Throw a six to start.

Fall down a ditch — miss a turn

**59**

**57**

Move ahead to number 58

**55**

**54**

Follow wrong sign — go back to number 32

Struck by lightning. Throw a 6 to restart

You are granted a wish — have a free turn

**52**

**29**

**32**

Lost in the forest — miss a turn

**28**

Rest for a while — miss a turn

Tree falls across your path. Throw a 3 to restart

**27**

Swim across river to number 32

**24**

**35**

**23**

**22**

**21**

Lost in long grass. Miss a turn

**19**

**START**

**2**

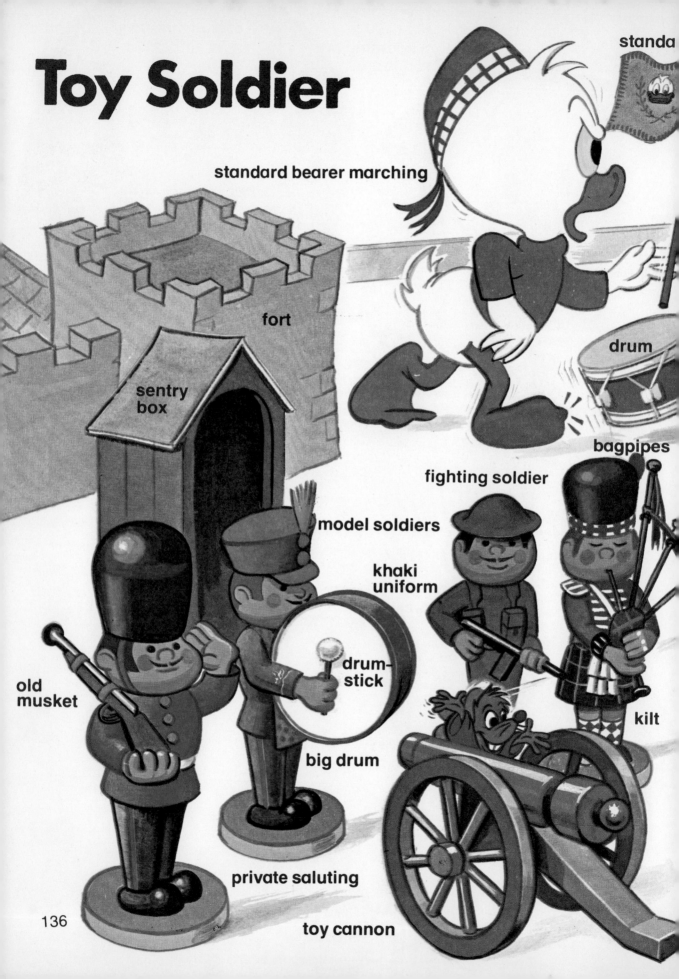

# Toy Soldier

standa

standard bearer marching

fort

drum

sentry box

bagpipes

fighting soldier

model soldiers

khaki uniform

drum-stick

old musket

kilt

big drum

private saluting

toy cannon

tin helmet

a bearskin hat too large

playing soldiers

sergeant stripes

standing at attention

medal

gun turret

toy tank

bomb

wooden sword

tank tracks

a tank attack!

key

bugle

137

crows' nest

farmer

silo

barn

cow

farmer's
wife

hayrick

cowshed

fierce bull

# Farmer

ow

hedge

combine harvester

cornfield

farmhouse

tractor

baler

bale of hay

gate

startled chicken

wall

silly picnickers who left the gate open

weeds

139

# Astronaut

first stage

second stage

third stage

sky rocket

weightless astronauts

Earth

space helmet

space suit

space walk

moon-landing vehicle

satellite

antenna

Moon

American flag

moon dust

crater

moon buggy

140

parachutes

rescue helicopter

control capsule

splash-down in the sea

control room

tv monitors

QDD-3

controls

computers

controller

dials

control panel

switches

141

# Police

bulletin board

police station

Police Ball
Fri: 7:30

Found

Wanted

Burglar Bill

reward notice

policewoman

cap

policeman on
desk duty

policeman's club

handcuffs

chair

burglar

alert bloodhound

142

police car

special
detective

pencil

notepad

private eye

cell

prisoner

stray dog

bars

dog bowl

143

# Nurse

adhesive tape

bandaged head

splint

stethoscope

disinfectant

cotton

PLUTO

144

ambulance

AMBULANCE

...ident

nurse's cap

Red Cross nurse

nurse's watch

roll of tape

starched apron

first aid bag

...ummified ...tient

ointment

scissors

cough medicine

spoon

pills

# Cowboy

small western town

barn

hitching post

cactus

guard

stage coach

money bag

gun

bandit

dust

wheel

horse

stirrup

146

147

# Roadwork

workman's shelter

pick-axe

equipment box

burst pipe

trench

spade

manhole

rake

drain pipe

tar spreader

sticky boots

hot tar

148

smoke

smoke stack

red flag

road block

tar boiler

road lamp

roller

steam roller

tar

wheelbarrow

tools left in tar

kettle

brazier

warm toes

lunch-break

149

# Blacksmith

horseshoes

horse to be shod

rider

cartwheel

anvil

horsecollar

owner of horse

block

hooves

shoeing knife

pincers

chimney

hood

blacksmith

tongs

hand bellows

leather apron

hot coke

very hot horseshoe

rasp

forge

wooden pail

hammer

horseshoe nails

151

# Golfer

greenskeeper

mower

golfer in rough

fore!

wooden club

golfer

golfing jacket

putter

bunker

studs

golf shoe

crow stealing ball

club flag

clubhouse

flag

water

golfer finding ball

caddie

green

golf umbrella

hole

orm

golf bag

grass

tee marker

N°4

cart

# Fire

smoke

water jet

alarm bell

fire escape

fire buckets

fire engine arriv
at the scene

154

flames

lady in distress

fireman to the rescue

fireman's helmet

boots

OFFICE

re bell

axe to
break door down

ladder

water hose

water
hydrant

valve

155

# Band

trombone

concertin[a]

piano

sheet music

pianist

cello

broken
cello string

velvet bow-tie

keys

mu
sc

foot pedal

saxophone

violin

violin bow

sousaphone

triangle

paper airplane
(not a musical
instrument!)

drumsticks

drum

mskin

conductor

foot tapping in time to the music

music
stand

rostrum

# What's Wrong?

1

3

4

What is wrong
with each of
the pictures?